HISTORY OF
EUROPE

Brian Dicks

Wayland

EUROPE

Series Editor: Janet De Saulles
Book Editor : Liz Wyse
Series Design: Bridgewater Design
Book Design: Jackie Berry

First published in 1992 by Wayland (Publishers) Ltd.,
61, Western Road, Hove, BN3 1JD, England

© Copyright 1992 Wayland (Publishers) Ltd.

British Library Cataloguing in Publication Data

Dicks, Brian
    History of Europe. – (Europe Series)
    I. Title II. Series
    940

ISBN 0-7502-0334-X

Typeset by Dorchester Typesetting Group Ltd.
Printed in Italy by G. Canale C.S.p.A., Turin
Bound in France by A.G.M.

ACKNOWLEDGEMENTS

Associated Press/Topham 27, 37, 38; The Bridgeman Art Library
26; British Museum 21; Department of Environment 25; C. M. Dixon 16,
30, 35; Werner Forman Archive 15; Dennis Hughes-Gilbey 3, 22, 23;
Sonia Halliday photographs 12, (Laura Lushington) 18, 34; Michael
Holford 12, 14, 23; Hutchinson Library 8, 21, 32, 44 (Leslie Woodhead) 15,
24, 32 (Christine Pemberton) 17 Bernard Régent 33, 37; The Mansell
Collection 25; Popperfoto/Reuter 6; Topham Picture Library 41; Wayland
Picture Library 28, 29, (Tim Sharman) 36; Zefa Picture Library (UK) Ltd. 11

Contents

Introduction: states and nations

Compared to other world land masses, such as Asia, Africa and the Americas, the area of Europe is relatively small. It accounts for only one-twelfth of the habitable earth, yet the remarkable fact is that Europe contains a quarter of the world's states or independent countries.

Europe's states fit together along irregular coastal and inland boundaries, like a giant political jigsaw. But the pieces of this jigsaw are neither of the same shape, nor of the same size. Some states, such as the Vatican City, San Marino, Andorra, Gibraltar and even Malta, are so small that they are no more than dots on the European map. In contrast, Europe has some very large countries, such as France, Spain, Germany and, especially, some of the countries which once made up the USSR (now the CIS).

Europe's changing map

Europe's political map is the result of hundreds of years of history, and the many boundary changes caused by migrations, colonizations, local conquests, widespread wars, peace treaties, the growth and decline of empires and nationalist movements. European boundaries are still altering and the most recent developments have been caused by the breakdown of communism. This has led to the reunification of Germany and the re-establishment of independent states in what was once Yugoslavia and the USSR.

Europe's nations

Europe's political geography is

Arctic Ocean

ICELAND

FINLAND

NORWAY

SWEDEN

Ural Mountains

ESTONIA

RUSSIA

NORTHERN
IRELAND

SCOTLAND

North Sea

DENMARK

LATVIA

REPUBLIC OF
IRELAND

LITHUANIA

Baltic Sea

UNITED KINGDOM

WALES

ENGLAND

BYELORUSSIA

NETHERLANDS

Atlantic Ocean

BELGIUM

GERMANY

POLAND

LUXEMBOURG

UKRAINE

Caspian
Sea

FRANCE

CZECHOSLOVAKIA

LIECHTENSTEIN

AUSTRIA

SWITZERLAND

HUNGARY

MOLDAVIA

ITALY

ROMANIA

GEORGIA

PORTUGAL

ANDORRA

MONACO

YUGOSLAVIA

Black Sea

SAN MARINO

SPAIN

VATICAN CITY

BULGARIA

ALBANIA

TURKEY

GIBRALTAR

Mediterranean Sea

GREECE

MALTA

CYPRUS

Map showing all the states and nations of Europe.

even more complicated than the map (*above*) indicates. This is because most of the states shown contain within their boundaries groups of people who regard themselves as separate nations.

The word nation is not the same as state, and Europe has many examples of multi-national states, such as Switzerland and Yugoslavia. In the former there are few problems, but in the latter

there have been great difficulties between national groups.

A nation is a group of people who are conscious of their individuality, or differences from other people. In other words they are conscious of their nationality. This is usually based on sharing a language or religion, or merely common traditions and ambitions. Many nations want complete independence, that is, separatism,

A rally in Lithuania in April 1990 supports calls for independence.

whereas others want only a greater involvement in running their affairs. This is known as autonomy and is found in the federal system of government.

The map (*below*) shows those parts of Europe where there are problems with national groups. The reasons for many of these problems lie deep in European history, but others have been caused by modern changes to Europe's map. Political boundaries have frequently been violated: smaller states, or parts of states, have been swallowed up by larger ones, and nations have been split between two or more states. Another movement among nations is one called irredentism. This means the reuniting of states – both people and territories – which existed in the past.

Today, the main talk in Europe is of greater economic and political unity. At the same time, however, there are many factors bringing about further political fragmentation. It has been said that if continents have specialisms, then Europe's is its political complexity. The following pages will try to make this complexity a little easier to understand.

This map shows the areas of Europe where there are problems with nationalist groups.

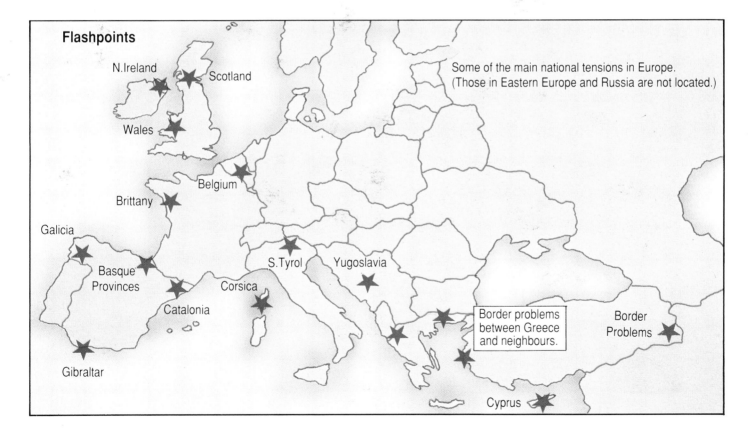

Flashpoints

Some of the main national tensions in Europe. (Those in Eastern Europe and Russia are not located.)

N.Ireland
Scotland
Wales
Belgium
Brittany
Galicia
S.Tyrol
Yugoslavia
Basque Provinces
Corsica
Catalonia
Gibraltar

Border problems between Greece and neighbours.

Border Problems

Cyprus

The first European civilizations

Europe is surrounded by water on three sides only: the Atlantic Ocean to the west, the Arctic Ocean to the north, and the Mediterranean Sea to the south. In the east, Europe is physically joined to Asia to form the giant continental area of Eurasia. The boundaries which geographers have used to distinguish Europe from Asia are complex. They follow the Ural Mountains, the Ural River, the Caspian Sea, the Caucasus Mountains, the Black Sea and the narrow sea channels (the Turkish Straits) linking the Black Sea with the Mediterranean. These boundaries have never been political, and there are many who regard them as unimportant, especially where they divide states between different continents.

Europe's shape

From its widest north-south extent, along its borders with Asia, Europe narrows westwards as it pushes towards the Atlantic. Its coastal outline is multi-peninsula, with a complicated mixture of promontories, local seas, gulfs, bays and channels, and numerous offshore islands, some forming archipelagos. This detailed interpenetration of land and sea has given Western Europe its maritime outlook and character. Initially in Mediterranean areas, and then along the Atlantic and Baltic coasts, its peoples developed a lively interest in trade. Eventually this was to lead to the establishment of overseas colonies and a flourishing world commerce.

Much of Eastern Europe did not share these trading advantages. Instead, its economy was to remain basically

The Atlantic coastline of Europe, with its bays, harbours and navigable rivers, has shaped the history of the peoples of Western Europe, encouraging trade and exploration.

agricultural, and its many different nations came under the control of large empires. Here there was little chance of individual government until these empires were overthrown by wars or revolutions. Even then, East and West Europe were to remain separate. Though there are no physical barriers, the boundary, until recently, was a political and economic one, separating the capitalist from communist countries.

Earliest peoples

The fact that Europe is joined to Asia has had an important impact on Europe's history. There have

Europe's Languages

Romance Group
Germanic group
Slavic group
Celtic group
Baltic group
Thraco-Illyrian
Hellenic
Non-Indo-European

Icelandic

Faeroese

Lappish
Lappish
Karelian
Finnish
Norwegian
Swedish
Estonian
Russian
Latvian
Lithuanian
Russian
Byelorussian
Gaelic
Danish
Erse
Welsh
English
Frisian
Low
Dutch
Flemish
Middle
German
Polish
Ukrainian
Breton
Langue d'Oil
High
Czech
French
Basque
Hungarian
Galician
Langue d'Oc
Italian
Slovenian
Romanian
Portuguese
Catalan
Serbo-Croatian
Bulgarian
Castillian Spanish
Albanian
Macedonian
Vlakh
Sardegnan
Greek

The complex mosaic of language groups within Europe can be seen on this map.

9

been movements of peoples in both directions, but it is from Asia that most early colonists and conquerors came. The most important land route was through the Eurasian Steppelands, reaching Europe to the north of the Caspian and Black Seas. Prehistoric peoples entered Europe along this route, bringing the domesticated horse. They also brought with them the Indo-European language from which most of Europe's present languages have developed.

Another very important westward route into Europe was from the Middle East through the Mediterranean Sea. Europe thus received many new economic and social ideas from more advanced peoples who had already developed sophisticated civilizations in parts of the Middle East. Among these new ideas and innovations were farming skills, based on animal domestication and crop cultivation. First practised around 3000 BC in the eastern Mediterranean, this new lifestyle took many hundreds of years to reach the Atlantic seaboard. Replacing Europe's hunting and collecting economies, farming was aided by other new inventions and technologies, particularly the change from stone tools and weapons to those made from metals, first copper and bronze, then the all-powerful iron.

The Celts

Present-day Europeans are the product of many successive peoples, not least the Celts. These Iron Age tribes influenced many parts of Europe from the eighth century BC onwards. Originally from Asia, they occupied the area from the upper Danube to the middle Rhine valleys. From here they moved into Iberia, the Balkans, France and the British Isles. They were efficient farmers and soldiers, and developed a rich artistic and religious culture.

Many river names in Europe – Rhine, Danube, Seine and Thames – are Celtic in origin, indicating the importance of Celtic culture. Although the Celts were eventually overcome by other European peoples, they are still found in Europe's western extremities, such as Brittany, Wales, Ireland and Scotland. Celtic traditions are also strong in Galicia (north-west Spain) and adjacent parts of Portugal. With shared histories and their native languages still spoken in many areas (in Wales especially), the Celts regard themselves as true nations and many want independence.

For these early times, we can only speak of political geography in very general terms. The early farming communities were probably organized into tribes who occupied lands they regarded as their own. They shared a common language and ancestry, and also loyalty to a leader. This earliest type of territorial organization in

Western and Central Europe was best developed by the Celtic peoples.

Crete and Greece

Europe's first state arose on the large Aegean island of Crete. This was long before the time the Celts and other peoples discovered farming. Crete acted as a natural stepping-stone between Asia, Africa and Europe, and after 2000 BC a rich Bronze Age civilization, called the Minoan (after the mythical King Minos), developed around palace-cities like Knossos. Minoan Crete was a powerful maritime state which ruled many parts of the east Mediterranean. But it was from the sea that its destruction came, in about 1250 BC, in the form of conquerors and natural disaster.

These conquerors were the Greeks who had moved from the mainland into the Aegean islands. From the sixth century BC onwards they made Greece the main centre of European civilization, and it is impossible to even list the great advances they made in science, philosophy, art, literature and architecture. In addition, the Greeks experimented with forms of government and gave us such words as monarchy, aristocracy and, of course, democracy.

The Greeks developed a political unit called the *polis* or city-state. Each polis consisted of

an independent, self-governing city and its surrounding farms and villages. Numerous city-states sprang up in the Greek mainland and Aegean islands. All were proud of their Greek heritage but they also jealously guarded their sovereignty. One of the most influential was Athens, and it was here that democracy, or government by the people, was born in the fifth century BC.

Traders and colonists

The Greeks also influenced Europe as traders and colonists. They founded many cities around the shores of the Black and Mediterranean Seas and Plato likened them to 'ants and frogs around a pool'. Among these

The Acropolis was the military and religious heart of Classical Athens. It is still dominated today by the Parthenon temple.

Above **Alexander the Great, who took Greek civilization to the borders of India, is depicted defeating the Persians.**

THE ROMAN EMPIRE

The Roman Empire grew from humble beginnings in the Latium area of central Italy. Here Rome started as a collection of hilltop villages which grew in size and united in the eighth century BC to form one settlement.

The Romans first expanded their territory in the Italian peninsula, conquering the Etruscans to the north, and the Greek cities to the south. Developing a powerful navy, it was not long before they conquered all the lands surrounding the Mediterranean Sea. Here their main enemies had long been the

colonial cities were Byzantium (modern Istanbul), Neapolis (Naples), and Masilia (Marseilles) which had important trading links with the western Celts.

Ancient Greece was divided into small city-states. This meant it was easy prey for conquering outsiders. The main Mediterranean competitors of the Greeks were the Phoenicians, whose original homeland was in the east, the narrow coastal plain of Lebanon and Syria.

To the west, the Greeks also faced the military and commercial competition of the Etruscans, who had developed a rich civilization in the area of Italy between the rivers Arno and Tiber. All three powers would ultimately face the might of Rome.

Right **This equestrian statue of Marcus Aurelius (AD161-180) proclaims the empire's power and military might.**

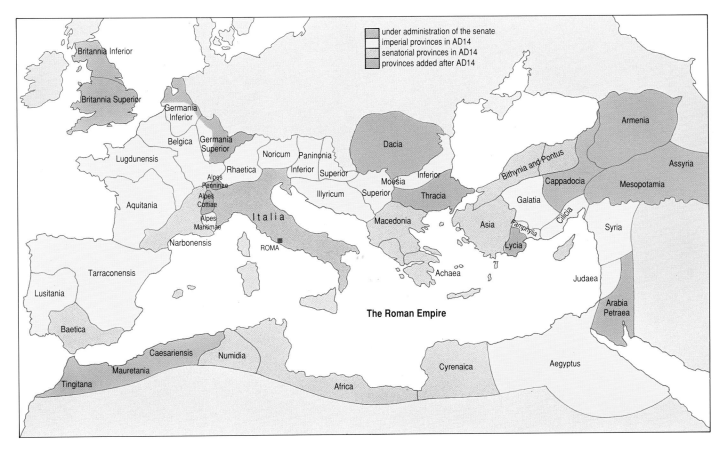

Legend:
- under administration of the senate
- imperial provinces in AD14
- senatorial provinces in AD14
- provinces added after AD14

Britannia Inferior

Britannia Superior

Germania Inferior

Belgica

Germania Superior

Lugdunensis

Noricum

Paninonia

Rhaetica

Inferior

Superior

Alpes Penninae

Alpes Cottiae

Alpes Maritimae

Aquitania

Italia

ROMA

Narbonensis

Tarraconensis

Lusitania

Baetica

Caesariensis

Numidia

Mauretania

Tingitana

Africa

Illyricum

Dacia

Moesia

Superior

Inferior

Thracia

Macedonia

Achaea

Asia

Pamphylia

Lycia

Bithynia and Pontus

Galatia

Cappadocia

Cilicia

Armenia

Assyria

Mesopotamia

Syria

Judaea

Arabia Petraea

Cyrenaica

Aegyptus

The Roman Empire

The Roman Empire at its greatest extent covered a vast area.

Carthaginians, who were of Phoenician origin. They were finally defeated by the Romans in 146 BC, when the city of Carthage was destroyed.

Mare nostrum

Without question, the Mediterranean was the centre of the empire's political and economic unity. The Romans proudly called it *mare nostrum* (`our sea'). As well as being an important trading route, it was also a way by which peoples and ideas moved between the empire's eastern and western parts. The Greek or Hellenic lands of the eastern Mediterranean had a strong influence on the Romans. Greek ideas of democracy, science and the arts completely changed the early Roman way of life.

As well as controlling the Mediterranean lands, the Roman Empire also covered a large part of western and central Europe. The Roman army maintained order and security, providing a period of relative peace which came to be known as the *Pax Romana*. This enabled civilized life to flourish beyond the Mediterranean, and towns were built where they had never existed before.

Among the many hundreds of European towns founded by the Romans are Cologne, London, Lyons, Koblenz and Mainz. Many were built close to navigable rivers and their inhabitants were engaged in trade, manufacturing, administration and other urban pursuits. To connect their towns, the Romans constructed a well-engineered road system which also served their many frontier forts and other military defences.

A multinational state

Although it is called an empire, the territory governed from Rome was a massive multinational state. It reached its maximum size in the first century AD when it extended from the Persian Gulf to the Scottish Borders and from the Strait of Gibraltar to the Caucasus Mountains. In Europe alone it was made up of numerous ethnic groups, including the many Celtic tribes of Britain and Gaul (France), the Iberians of Spain and Portugal, the Illyrian and Greek peoples of the Balkans and the Germanic tribes along the Rhine frontier.

For a long time this single political entity was held together by a large and efficient army, and by a sound administration. This was organized at both provincial level and centrally from Rome. The saying that 'all roads led to Rome' was a true one. Administrative control was also greatly helped by

Many Roman engineering works – roads, aqueducts, bridges – still survive today. The Pont du Gard aqueduct in France, built in the first century AD, was 270 metres long.

Right **Rome was protected from barbarian invasions by a border of walls, forts and ditches such as Hadrian's Wall, which stretches 117km along the Scottish border.**

the use of a *lingua franca* ('common language'), which was Latin, named after the first Romans of Latium. It became widely understood in the Romanized parts of Western and Central Europe and North Africa.

The empire's division

Beyond the empire itself was the world of the barbarian peoples. The word barbarian was used to describe those who could not speak the Classical languages, Greek or Latin, and were therefore outside the realm of civilized life. Increasingly, Rome came under pressure from these peoples.

From the third century on, the Roman Empire weakened. This was the result of both internal troubles and external pressures on its borders. For military and

Below **The Forum was the political centre of Ancient Rome.**

administrative convenience it was divided in AD 395 into two parts. The eastern part was ruled by an emperor at Byzantium, which was renamed Constantinople (nowadays called Istanbul), and the western part by an emperor ruling from Rome, but sometimes from Milan, Ravenna or Trèves. The fates of these various empires were very different. The Eastern Empire, where Greek culture prevailed, went on to become the Christian Byzantine Empire. It continued as a political power until being finally overthrown by the Ottoman Turks in 1453. The Western Empire which included Italy, Iberia (roughly corresponds to area occupied by Spain and Portugal), Gaul, Britain and North Africa, was far less successful. In the fifth century it collapsed under the pressure of barbarian conquests. These peoples were to play an extremely important part in the future political reshaping of Europe.

The folk migrations

The collapse of the Roman Empire in Western Europe opened wide the floodgates to barbarian peoples. They crossed the frontiers in large numbers in search of richer lands. These movements, not just of armies but of whole colonizing peoples, are known as the 'barbarian invasions'. But a better word is the German one *Völkerwanderung*, meaning 'folk wandering'.

The Germanic or Teutonic peoples were the first to move. They were followed by the Slavs, then peoples from Asia and North Africa. As a result of these conquests and settlements many of the patterns of European states and nations began to emerge. In place of the extensive and unified Roman Empire, a large number of independent countries developed in both the former Romanized lands and in areas beyond the frontiers.

Germania

The earliest known homeland of the Germans – the land the Romans called *Germania* on their maps – was the area between the lower Rhine and lower Oder rivers, together with the Danish peninsula and islands, and southern Sweden. Traditionally the German tribes were stock-rearers and fisherfolk who lived in difficult environments

The Ostrogothic chief, Theodoric the Great, invaded Italy in 488, and was buried in Roman style in this mausoleum in Ravenna.

such as forest, heath and marsh. In time, some were encouraged to settle in Roman lands, and the empire's army also depended on Germanic mercenaries, that is, soldiers hired to fight, often against their own people.

Many tribes, especially those with similar dialects and common traditions, grouped themselves into powerful confederations. It was their conquests which were largely responsible for the final destruction of Roman rule in Western Europe.

The island of Lindisfarne in Northumbria was an early English monastic community. Many English missionaries travelled to Europe from England.

The Franks

By the third and fourth centuries the most powerful Germanic nations in Western Europe were the Goths, Alemans, Burgundians and Franks. In addition there were the Angles, Saxons and Jutes who colonized Southern Britain. Of all these peoples, the Franks played the most important part in shaping the political geography of Western Europe. They are first mentioned in the third century when they lived close to the Rhine frontier, between the Roman fortress towns of Cologne and Mainz. This area, on the river's right bank, down to its estuary, was known as Francia. Many Franks had already settled in Roman lands across the frontier, and others served in the Roman legions. They were the most Romanized of the Germanic nations and were able to occupy further lands when the empire began to crumble.

This window from Chartres cathedral in France commemorates scenes from the life of Charlemagne.

By the fifth century the Franks were divided into two main confederations. The East Franks moved from the Rhinelands into the areas of Westphalia, Hesse and further east towards the Thuringian Forest. Here they came into contact with other Germanic confederations, such as the Alemans and Thuringians, but the early kingdoms they founded did not last. The West Franks were far more successful. Crossing the Rhine they settled much of the Low Countries and then took over Roman Gaul, north of the Loire river and east of Celtic Brittany. They became most powerful under the leadership of Clovis who ruled the Franks from 481-511. The Frankish (Merovingian) dynasty lasted from the fifth to the eighth centuries. By then their territory extended to the Pyrenees; the Visigoths (West Goths) controlled much of Iberia.

Although the West Franks kept many of their Germanic traditions, they also became more thoroughly Romanized. Instead of speaking a German dialect, they came to use a Latin dialect which developed into French. In addition, they accepted the Roman Catholic faith, and the Merovingian kings were strongly supported by the Pope in all their territorial conquests and claims. In return they became protectors of the Pope. This relationship between Crown and Church, sometimes friendly but often antagonistic, became an important feature of political life in Medieval Europe.

The Carolingian Empire

In the middle of the eighth century the Frankish empire came under the control of the Carolingians, a dynasty whose most famous leader was Charlemagne (Charles the Great). He became king of the Franks in 771 and extended his Empire's boundaries eastwards, and also southwards into Italy. Here he defeated the Lombards, Germanic peoples who threatened Rome and the Church. In gratitude for his protection Pope Leo III crowned Charlemagne Emperor of the West Romans in 800.

In Italy and in other parts of the Carolingian Empire, frontier areas were defended by border *marches* (buffer zones). Further control came from the *Kaiserpfalzen*, or imperial strongholds, such as Worms, Ingelheim, Nijmwegen and the royal capital of Aachen. As well as being important trading centres these and other towns, Aachen especially, were also centres of European learning. Under Charlemagne there was a revival of Greek and Roman scholarship, and his empire had many contacts with Anglo-Saxon Britain. Here a similar cultural 'renaissance' was taking place, especially during the reign of Alfred the Great (871-99).

Map showing the extent of Charlemagne's empire in 814. It also shows the lines of its subsequent division between his three grandsons.

WALES

ENGLAND

Frisia

Saxony

Francia

Austrasia

Neustria

The Carolingian Empire *East Franks*

Bavaria

West Franks

Alemannia

Carinthia

Lotharingia

Friuli

Aquitania

Burgundy

Gascony

Provence

Septimania

Kingdom of Lombardy

Division after Charlemagne's death

KINGDOM OF S.ITALY AND SICILY

The legacy of Charlemagne

Charlemagne died in 814, and the land squabbles which followed his death led to the Treaty of Verdun in 843. The Emperor's territory was partitioned between his three grandsons, and the kingdoms they received had lasting effects on Europe's political map.

Charles was given the western kingdom (*see map, page* 19) which became the basis of the present French state. Louis received lands to the east of the Rhine and this became German territory, which grew greatly by eastward expansion. Between the two was the elongated middle kingdom given to Lothar, and known as Lotharingia. It stretched from Italy, across the Alps and along the Rhône-Saône Corridor, and part of the Rhine valley to the North Sea.

Lotharingia proved impossible to defend or unite, and quickly became the zone of conflict between its more powerful neighbours, France and Germany. Conflict both over, and within, Lotharingia has continued right down to the present century.

THE GROWTH OF FRANCE

France is the largest state by area in Western Europe, and it is also one of the oldest. Its present boundaries are almost identical to those of Roman Gaul, but in the ninth century French territory was considerably smaller. As well as its coastal boundaries, from the Mediterranean to the English Channel, France has always wanted natural land boundaries, such as the Pyrenees which separate it from Spain. In the east,

France has always regarded the Alps, the Jura and the Rhine as its so-called *limites naturelles*, as these were also the boundaries of Roman Gaul.

Soon after the Verdun treaty the kingdom given to Charles became split into numerous quarrelling kingdoms or feudal lordships. The local lords paid only lip-service to the king and they governed their lands as fully independent rulers. For a long time, this political disunity would prevent France from successfully pushing its borders eastwards into other lands

In 987, the empty title of king passed to the Capets. Their royal estates, or *demense* lands were concentrated in a strip of territory in the centre of the Paris Basin. Called the Île-de-France, this had been the earlier capital of the West Franks.

With the help of the Church, the Capetian kings gained control over lands outside the royal demense. This was achieved through arranged marriages, legal inheritances, purchases and confiscations. Steadily, the royal lands increased in size and the Paris Basin became the nucleus, around which modern France emerged to become one of Europe's most unified and centralized states.

Above **Notre Dame de Paris. Founded by the Romans, Paris has always been the political and cultural capital of France.**

Below **Peasants work in a French nobleman's fields.**

Old women in Brittany, wearing the traditional Breton headdress, are a reminder of the region's distinctive customs and traditions.

Disruptive forces in France

These do, and have always existed. As expected, they are mainly confined to France's borders. For example, Brittany, which occupies the north-western peninsula, still retains the Breton language and distinctive customs.

These date from c. 500 when it was settled by Celtic peoples from Britain. The Celtic tongue is still spoken, mainly in rural areas, and this forms the basis of separatist, national claims.

At France's Atlantic end of the Pyrenees are people who speak Basque, a language whose origin is unknown. Most Basques, however, are found across the Spanish border, where their movement for an independent state is much more vigorous, and frequently violent. The Catalans are also divided between France and Spain, at the Mediterranean end of the Pyrenees. Their fight for separatism is again more active in Spain.

Today, the main challenge to total French unity comes from the Mediterranean island of Corsica. In 1768 it was sold to France by the Italian city state of Genoa, and since this time the Corsicans have felt betrayed and fought for their independence. They, too, have their own language, a dialect of Italian rather than French.

Capetian control was made difficult by the large amount of France which belonged to England. When Henry Plantagenet came to the English throne in 1154, he inherited the whole of north-western France – Normandy, Brittany, Maine, Anjou and Tourraine. In addition, his marriage to Eleanor of Aquitaine gave him much of south-western France. The area of France ruled by the English was thus far larger than that ruled by the French. Inevitably, wars between the two countries were continuous, but the English were finally evicted from all of France (except Calais) in 1453. Later they also lost Calais, retaining only the Channel Islands.

Another territorial struggle of the French kings was with the Burgundians. These Germanic peoples had built the powerful state of Burgundy in the area stretching from Dijon, south to

Lyons and including the Alpes Maritimes. By the fourteenth century they were in firm control of the lucrative trade route through the Rhône-Saône Corridor, which linked the Paris Basin with the Mediterranean. The French rulers defeated Burgundy in the sixteenth century and annexed its land. This brought France's south-eastern boundaries deep into Lotharingia, with its *limites naturelles* extending through the Alps, and the Jura.

By the year 1700, France had gained most of its present territory and political boundaries. Within them a remarkable degree of national unity developed. This was partly the result of geographical factors, including the compact shape of French territory, its naturally-defined borders, and the presence of a dominant core area, the Paris region, which continues to influence this highly centralized European state. The French language has also been a major unifying factor.

THE GROWTH OF GERMANY

Unlike France, Germany is one of Europe's more recent states. The size and shape of this country has greatly changed, especially since 1871 when the modern German Empire was founded. These changes in boundaries brought Germany into conflict with France and other western countries and also with the Slavic nations of Eastern Europe.

The part of Charlemagne's empire given to Louis covered approximately the area of the modern Federal Republic of Germany. Known as U*rdeutschland,*

Above **Avignon, southern France. Between 1307 and 1377, the papacy was moved from Rome to Avignon.**

Below **Part of the Bayeux tapestry, depicting the Norman conquest of England, which brought Saxon rule to an end.**

it had kept its original German population during the great westward movement of peoples between 400 and 900. It became the area of the revived Holy Roman Empire which, however, was united for a very short time only. Instead there was great political fragmentation, and by the 1600s Germany had more than 300 separate states. To further complicate matters, these states were often split into many separate parts. The empire

The Slavs

Like the Germans, the Slavic peoples played an important part in Europe's *Völkerwanderung*. Their original home was probably somewhere in the Ukraine and Byelorussia in the east, from where they moved in all directions into Europe. They, too, have left an important imprint on Europe's map of nations and states. Today they make up one-third of Europe's people, and about one-twelfth of the world's population. The Slavs are divided into eastern, western and southern groups. Slavic languages included Great Russian, White Russian (Byelorussian), Ukrainian, Bulgarian, Czech, Slovak, Serbo-Croat, Slovene and Polish.

The Slavic peoples have been called Europe's 'soft anvil', exposed to the hard blows of two great hammers. One has been the mounted nomads who came out of Asia, and the other has been the German pioneers and colonists from the west.

Opposite page **The magnificent Gothic cathedral in Cologne, begun in 1248.**

Right **Otto von Bismarck, the chief minister of Prussia.**

Below **A German manuscript illustration of a besieged castle.**

survived in name only until 1806. Its hereditary rulers were the Habsburgs, whose role as emperors was merely ceremonial. The unification of Germany's many small states took place in the nineteenth century and was largely the work of the German Chancellor, Otto von Bismarck.

Colonial Germany

The movement of the Germans into lands occupied by the Slavs had important effects on Europe's political geography. Called the D*rang nach Osten* ('the push eastward'), it took place from about 800 to 1400. The Germans came to Eastern Europe in search of agricultural land, to develop trade and industry in the eastern towns, and in some cases as Christian missionaries to the then pagan Slavs.

Many Germans migrated to parts of what are now Hungary, Romania and Russia, but much of their eastern settlement was confined to two main areas of expansion. One was along the Danube valley and into the eastern Alps, and the other was along the North German Plain and shores of the Baltic Sea. Surrounded by Slavs, both areas became march (German *mark*) provinces, the political borderlands which were to become the powerful German states and empires of Austria and Prussia.

25

Towards Waterloo and Sarajevo

During these formative times, from the fourteenth century onwards, Europe experienced many major cultural and political changes which profoundly affected its peoples, both individually and collectively. In particular, Europe's western countries came under the influence of both the Renaissance and the Reformation.

The Renaissance

This, the French word for re-birth, took place from the fourteenth to sixteenth centuries, and was a time of great cultural and intellectual revival. Classical Greek and Roman values were reintroduced to a Western Europe long under the control of medieval feudalism. Starting in Italy, the ideas and the innovations of the Renaissance spread throughout Western Europe, supported by the Church and by kings and nobles. Some of Europe's greatest artists, architects, scholars and scientists were living and working throughout this period.

The Reformation

Whereas the Renaissance was a uniting force, the Reformation was a divisive one. This religious movement to reform the Roman

During the Renaissance, art and architecture flourished in Italian cities such as Florence.

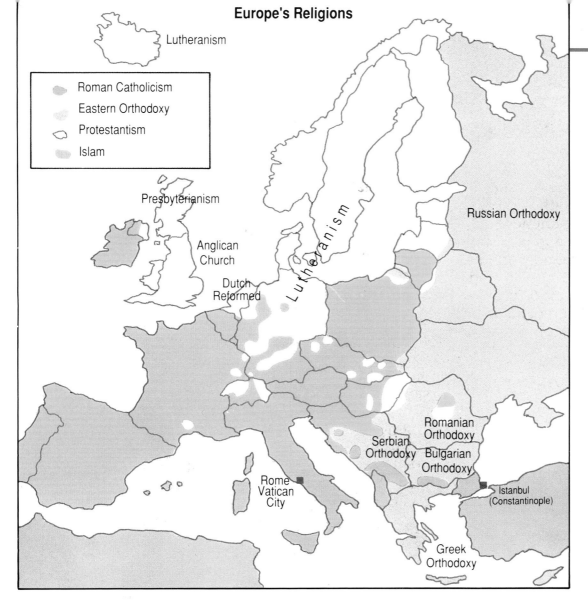

Europe's Religions

Lutheranism

- Roman Catholicism
- Eastern Orthodoxy
- Protestantism
- Islam

Presbyterianism

Anglican Church

Dutch Reformed

Lutheranism

Russian Orthodoxy

Romanian Orthodoxy

Serbian Orthodoxy

Bulgarian Orthodoxy

Rome Vatican City

Istanbul (Constantinople)

Greek Orthodoxy

Left **It can be seen from this map that Christianity is the main religion of Europe, although there are three main subdivisions.**

Catholic Church was begun in the sixteenth century by Martin Luther in Germany and John Calvin in France. It led to Protestantism, which stated that people had direct responsibility to God, rather than to Church authority. In England, Henry VIII rejected the power of the Pope and formed the Church of England. Similar rejections took place in the Netherlands, Denmark and parts of Germany, and soon much of Western Europe was involved in political and religious wars.

Fought mainly in Germany, but involving most Western and Northern European countries, the Thirty Years War (1618-48) devastated large areas. It began as a war between followers of the Catholic and Protestant religions, but then became a struggle to determine the power the Habsburgs (emperors of the Holy Roman Empire) wielded over

their subjects. At the end of the war, the Treaty of Westphalia greatly curbed their power, hence that of the Catholic Church. This gave the German kingdoms, notably Prussia, further opportunities to pursue their own political courses.

Age of Revolution

The French Revolution and its aftermath was to transform the map of Europe. It began in 1789 when the French middle classes rose up against the country's aristocracy and the outdated feudal system. The French monarchy was overthrown, but many countries rose to its defence, involving Europe in the French Revolutionary Wars (1792-1802). Out of these French campaigns came a brilliant general, Napoleon Bonaparte, born in Corsica in 1769. Not content merely to defend France, his ambition was to extend its frontiers far beyond the *limites naturelles*, not only eastwards but also into Britain. Napoleon reached Moscow in 1812, but the harsh Russian winters destroyed his armies which were forced to retreat. By now the rest of Europe was ready to challenge Napoleon, and the decisive battle was fought on June 18, 1815, near the small Belgian town of Waterloo. Here British and Prussian forces defeated Napoleon and his idea of a united Europe under the control of France. The German states, however, had their own ideas about the way in which Europe could come under their control.

EUROPE 1815-1914

Dramatic political changes took place in Europe during the hundred years following the Battle of Waterloo. Europe's political pattern in 1815 was drawn up by the Congress of Vienna, which met to settle the boundary problems left by the Napoleonic Wars. The territory of France was immediately pushed back to its *limites naturelles*, and a buffer zone was strengthened between France and Germany. Much of this area was the old Kingdom of Lotharingia, which was still divided between many small states. In 1815 it formed a complicated north-south zone, separating the large European empires further east from the Atlantic states of Britain,

Left **By 1812 Napoleon Bonaparte controlled the greater part of Western Europe. Defeated at Waterloo, he spent his last years in exile on the South Atlantic British island of St. Helena.**

Portugal, Spain and France. With the exception of the latter, these countries have had few boundary changes in their histories.

The buffer states

Many parts of Lotharingia continued to change hands, especially the area of Alsace-Lorraine, which stands astride the French-German language border.

To the north are the buffer states of Luxembourg and Belgium, which have tried to act as neutral territories between Germany and France. Luxembourg is a Grand Duchy, one of the last of the many small states once common to Lotharingia. It traces its origin back to 1354 and gained full independence in the latter part of the nineteenth century.

In 1866, Belgium was deliberately created as a 'buffer state' between France and Germany. This artificial creation of the 'Great Powers' was formed partly from lands which had belonged to the Netherlands, and partly from French territory. In the north people speak Flemish, and are known as Flemings, their language being a dialect of Dutch. In the south are the Walloons, who speak a French dialect. The boundary between these nations crosses Belgium to the south of Brussels which, to complicate matters further, is mainly a French-speaking city surrounded by a

Flemish countryside. Belgium has major nationalist problems, simply because it lies astride a linguistic and religious border.

Switzerland

Not all of Lotharingia has had problems with political groupings. Switzerland, one of Europe's oldest states, has kept its neutrality and organized its many different peoples, speaking different languages, into a federal multinational state.

Swiss independence began in the thirteenth century. The German rulers were eager to preserve their access routes through the Alpine passes, which led to the rich trading and religious cities of Italy. In return for defending these routes, the Swiss mountain peoples were freed from feudal duties. From this small nucleus of free peasants originally living in the 'Forest Cantons', grew the

This nineteenth-century children's jigsaw illustrates the nations of Europe and outlines certain national characteristics and pastimes.

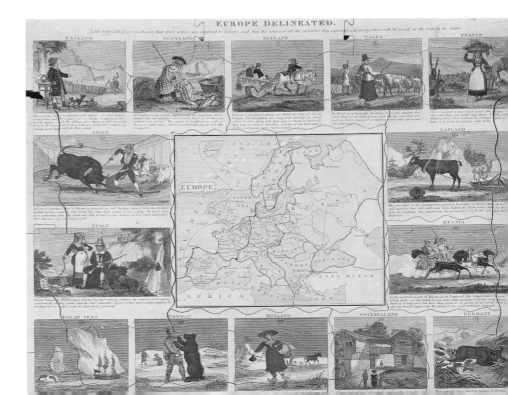

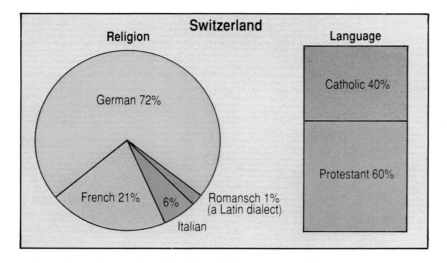

Switzerland

Religion

German 72%

French 21%

6%

Italian

Romansch 1%
(a Latin dialect)

Language

Catholic 40%

Protestant 60%

Swiss Confederation. All groups that joined the union, whatever their language and religion, had to agree to strict democratic principles. The Swiss wanted no part in building large states or empires. Neither did they wish to dominate any partners in the confederacy.

A rich European federal state of great cultural diversity developed, and Switzerland has sustained a shared state identity for almost seven centuries.

Italy

Between 1815 and 1914, some of the biggest changes to the political map of Western Europe took place in the areas which became the united countries of Italy and Germany. Despite its central importance to the Roman Empire, Italy had become a mosaic of states, largely as a result of conquests from the north.

Long before unification, Italy's north was politically linked to the Holy Roman Empire and the Austro-Hungarian Empire. It was an area of flourishing city states, such as Venice, Milan, Pisa, Florence, Genoa and Padua. In Italy's centre, based around Rome, was the rapidly diminishing area of the once powerful Papal States. Today they survive only as the Vatican City State. Italy's largest political unit was the southern kingdom of the Two Sicilies which combined southern Italy and the island of Sicily. It had been ruled successively by Arabs, Normans and Spanish.

Italy's unification took place in a short period of time – about ten years – much of it being achieved by 1870. The movement, called the *Risorgimento* ('Resurrection'), was led by Mazzini, Garibaldi and Cavour. It started in the country's Piemonte area (around modern Turin and Genoa), but this nuclear area lost its capital status to Rome – which had historical, locational and religious advantages.

Austria and Prussia

These countries and their empires came to dominate much of Europe's politics after 1815.

The chart (opposite) **shows Switzerland's religious and linguistic divisions.**

Opposite page **Statue of Garibaldi in Washington Square, New York.**

Below **Europe, 1815.**

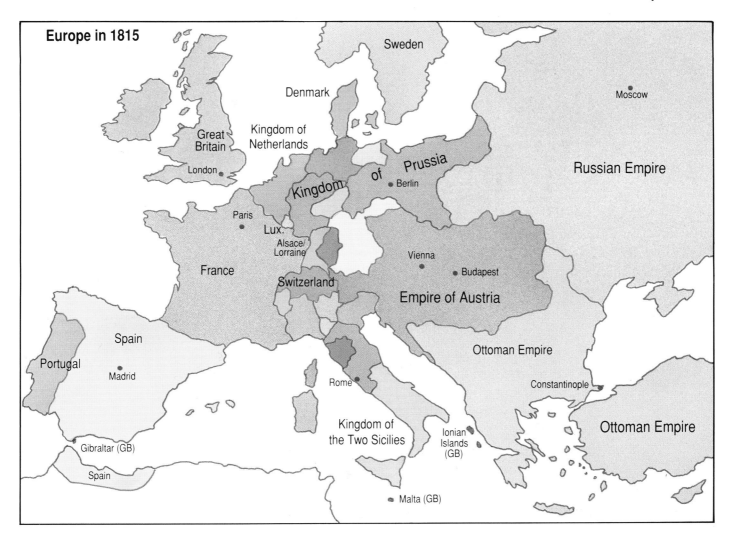

Europe in 1815

Sweden
Denmark
Moscow
Great Britain
London
Kingdom of Netherlands
Kingdom of Prussia
Berlin
Russian Empire
Paris
Lux.
Alsace/Lorraine
Vienna
France
Switzerland
Budapest
Empire of Austria
Spain
Portugal
Madrid
Ottoman Empire
Rome
Constantinople
Gibraltar (GB)
Spain
Kingdom of the Two Sicilies
Ionian Islands (GB)
Ottoman Empire
Malta (GB)

Spain's Moorish rulers built this palace-citadel (the Alhambra) at Granada.

Spain and Portugal

The large Iberian peninsula is shared by Spain, Portugal and the tiny British colony of Gibraltar. It is surrounded by sea on all sides except the north-east, where Spain's borders with France follow the Pyrenees. Here the small republic of Andorra is situated. Though Spain and Portugal have always had important links with the rest of Europe, the Pyrenees have acted as a barrier to contact. The Iberian peninsula was invaded by Islamic Moors in 711, and the Islamic religion held sway in most of Iberia until 1492, when the last outpost – the kingdom of Granada – was finally liberated (the *reconquista*). This long period of Islamic rule was to permanently change the character of Iberia, reinforcing its separation from the rest of Europe.

Much of Portugal's early history is similar to Spain's. But in the eleventh century, it became an independent country, with its first capital at Guimarães in the north. From here it expanded southwards, its boundaries with Spain being those between the Portuguese and Spanish languages. Despite much commercial rivalry during the Age of Discoveries, these boundaries have hardly changed since the thirteenth century.

Being a bigger country, Spain has always had more 'national' problems than Portugal. The creation of Madrid as a new central capital in 1561 was an attempt to unite Spain's historic regions. Today there are many groups seeking separatism, including the Basques and Catalans. Spain also has political problems with Britain over the ownership of Gibraltar.

The Schonbrünn palace in Vienna, the capital of the Austro-Hungarian empire.

They started as German *marks*; the Ostmark ('east *mark*') to the south eventually becoming the Habsburg empire of Austria, the Mark of Brandenburg in the north becoming the Kingdom of Prussia. Austria was ruled by the Habsburgs and in 1867 it combined with Hungary to form the powerful Austro-Hungarian Empire with its capitals at Vienna and Budapest.

Frequently at war with France and Austria, Prussia became an independent duchy in the seventeenth century. It grew powerful under Frederick the Great who transformed its capital, Berlin, into a great commercial and cultural centre. Prussia quickly grew, its territory extending from the Rhine, far along the Baltic coast, into present-day Poland and beyond. Becoming Germany's most powerful state, Prussia played a leading role in German unification. Its king, Wilhelm I, became the first *kaiser* (emperor) of Germany in 1871, and Prince Otto von Bismarck became its first chancellor.

Following the First World War, Prussia was reduced in size, and was finally dissolved in 1947, after the Second World War. The Austro-Hungarian Empire survived only until the end of the First World War in 1918. This war started in its territory, in the Bosnian capital of Sarajevo, with the assassination of Archduke Franz Ferdinand of Austria. This act unleashed a world war which would again politically reshape Europe.

Eastern Europe

Eastern Europe covers a broad belt of land and has a 'continental' climate, with winters getting progressively colder towards the Urals and beyond. Much of it is rolling plain, with coniferous forests, arable lands and grasslands. The latter are known as the Eurasian Steppe, and stretch eastwards from the Ukraine to Mongolia. Out of this harsher environment came numerous colonists and invaders in search of richer lands, some of them penetrating deep into Central and Western Europe.

As well as the most important colonists, the Slavs, there were many other nationalities which moved into Eastern Europe and affected its political geography. In 896, the Magyars, nomadic horse-people from the Steppe, swept westwards into the Danube plain and settled the land which came to be the core region of Hungary. Between 1167 and 1227 the Mongols arrived and, under the leadership of Ghengis Khan, invaded as far as Hungary and Poland. Subsequently, the Turks, first the Seljuks and then the Ottomans, moved into Anatolia and the Balkan peninsula.

As a result of this conquest and colonization, Eastern Europe has an even greater variety of

This sixteenth-century Turkish miniature shows invading Turkish troops encountering Hungarian resistance.

peoples than its Western counterpart. It has long been a great mixture of states and nations, all of them having a variety of languages and other national differences. About sixty per cent of all Eastern Europeans are Slavs, but they speak a wide variety of national languages. The remaining peoples are mostly Magyars (Hungarians), Romanians (whose language is descended from Latin), Albanians (whose language is probably a dialect of ancient Illyrian), and Germans (the remnants of the push eastward). Some of the minority groups include Turks, Jews and Gypsies.

An Eastern Lotharingia

As well as being the meeting point of a variety of languages, Eastern Europe also became the area of contact between Roman Catholicism, Eastern Orthodoxy, Protestantism and Islam. These linguistic and religious differences became the breeding grounds for conflict which led to the continual appearance, and disappearance, of small, weak states. As in Lotharingia, they were usually swallowed up by more powerful neighbours – in this part of Europe by empires such as the Prussian-German, the Russian, the Austro-Hungarian and the Ottoman. The latter two empires held their peoples together in an uneasy unity, and by the end of the nineteenth century many of their nationalities were again seeking independence.

Poland

The boundaries of Poland have continually expanded and contracted according to the whims of more powerful neighbours. Poland's political weakness has always been the result of its vulnerable situation in the North European Plain, with borders open to invaders on almost every side. This has made it one of Europe's most politically troubled states.

Poland is named after the Slavic tribe called the *Poljane*. From their home area around Gniezno (west of Warsaw), the *Poljane* had occupied an area equivalent to that of Poland today by the tenth century. This state, then Europe's largest, reached its 'Golden Age '

The Parliament building in Budapest was completed in 1902. It reflects the grandeur of the Austro-Hungarian Empire at that time.

Town hall in Lostyn, Poland. This Germanic architecture is widespread in parts of Poland which were once East Prussia.

to Warsaw, in the geographical centre of the country, failed to stop Poland being ruthlessly divided between these more powerful states, and sometimes altogether vanishing from Europe's map.

In spite of many centuries of oppression, Poland survived as a state. This has been due to the unity of its people, based on the Polish language, the strength of the Roman Catholic Church, and pride in a long history. It was in Poland that the Free Trade Union movement, 'Solidarity', stood up to communism. This greatly helped to pave the way for the new political freedom now found in Eastern Europe.

Russia

One of the main keys to the political geography of Eastern Europe is Russia.

Russia grew out of the small principality of Muscovy, which was founded in 1263 by Alexander Nevsky. It survived many raids by Mongols and other Asiatic peoples, and in 1400 Moscow became the fortress capital. From here expansion took place in all directions, though Russia was particularly interested in gaining more European territory.

Peter the Great, tsar of Russia (1682-1725) introduced a Westernization policy, taking parts of Poland, Sweden and some

between the fourteenth and sixteenth centuries. At this time its kings ruled over not only Poles, but also many Germans, Ukrainians, Byelorussians and Lithuanians.

This period of territorial importance was short-lived, for Poland came under pressure from Germany in the west and the Slavic threat of Russia in the east. The transference of the Polish capital

Above **The Moscow Kremlin is a walled area in the centre of the city, enclosing palaces and churches.**

Yugoslavia

Meaning 'land of the South Slavs', Yugoslavia has been a political experiment to unite into one federal state a variety of peoples. These are the Croats, Serbs, Bosnians, Macedonians and others, all with their own religious, historical and social traditions.

The name Yugoslavia was first used in 1929 when it replaced the title of Kingdom of the Serbs, Croats and Slovenes. This had been founded on the collapse of the Austro-Hungarian empire. The monarchy was abolished in 1943 and a socialist federal state, with its own brand of communism was formed in 1945. The country was held together by Marshal Tito, but since his death there has been great unrest between the country's nations. The main conflict has been between the Serbs and Croats. Though both speak similar languages, the Croats are Roman Catholic while the Serbs are Eastern Orthodox. Other problems involving religion are between the Christian and Moslem communities, the latter dating from the time when this part of the Balkans was part of the Ottoman Empire. In 1992 Yugoslavia ceased to exist as a federal state.

Ottoman lands in the process. The movement of the capital to St. Petersburg did not stop the growth of Moscow which, following the Russian Revolution in 1917, was restored as capital in 1918. It became the heart of the world's largest federal, but also most centralized state. Moscow was the seat of supreme power and authority over what became known as the Union of Soviet Socialist Republics (USSR).

The Russian Revolution had introduced the communist political system which, after the Second World War, came into great conflict with Western capitalist ideas. The main battleground between the two ideologies was Eastern Europe. Here the Soviet Union had gradually established a buffer zone of 'puppet' states from Poland to the border of Greece, whose loyalty to Moscow was maintained by a strong Soviet army. The major dramatic and widespread recent changes in Eastern Europe are discussed in the final chapter.

Left **Marshall Tito, pictured during the Second World War. He held Yugoslavia together in the post-war period.**

37

A united Europe

All ideas of European unity were shattered by the First World War (1914-18). Starting as power rivalries between the ruling families of Europe (all of whom were related), it quickly became total warfare between the Central Powers (Germany, Austro-Hungary and the Ottoman Turks), and the Allies. The latter included Britain, France, Russia, Belgium, Italy, some Balkan states, and the USA and Japan, who had joined the cause.

Claiming the loss of some ten million lives, the war was described as 'a crime against Europe', and many thought (wrongly, however) that it was the end of Europe as a major world power. After the war, the Versailles Settlement (1919) redrew many of Europe's political boundaries.

During the First World War men lived, fought and died in trenches.

The First World War had brought the Austro-Hungarian, Prussian and Ottoman Empires to an end, and in their places a series of newly independent Eastern European states came into being. They stretched from Finland in the north to Albania in the south, and were designed to act as a buffer zone between the possible future threats of German and Russian expansion – eastwards and westwards, respectively. The founding of the worldwide League of Nations (1920), dedicated to international co-operation and the preservation of peace, was an important result of Versailles, as were attempts to restore a balance of power between France and Germany, by creating a demilitarized zone in the Rhinelands.

Below **Europe in 1914, on the eve of the First World War.**

Europe in 1914

Norway
Sweden
Denmark
Moscow
Ireland
Great Britain
Netherlands
London
Russia
Berlin
Belgium
Germany
Lux.
Paris
Alsace/Lorraine
Vienna
Budapest
France
Switzerland
Empire of Austria-Hungary
Italy
Romania
Madrid
Serbia
Portugal
Montenegro
Bulgaria
Constantinople (Istanbul)
Rome
Spain
Albania
Greece
Ottoman Empire
Athens

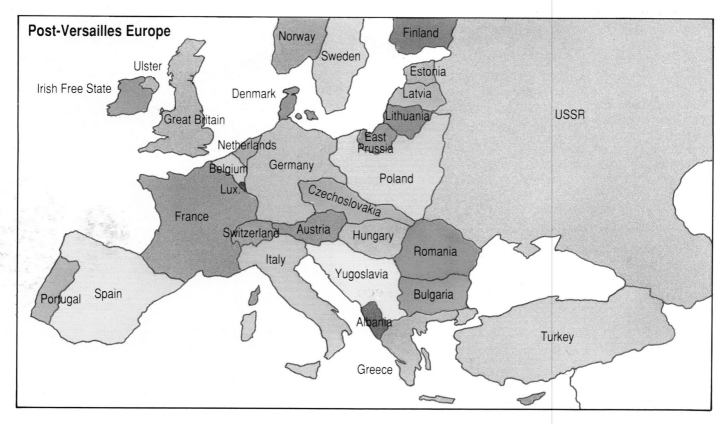

Post-Versailles Europe

The map of Europe drawn up after the Versailles peace conference (1919) left many dissatisfied minorities in Eastern Europe.

The Second World War

Versailles and other settlements were designed to prevent the future recurrence of war in Europe. But this was not to be, for the Second World War (1939-45) again brought catastrophe. It was the result of German aggression under the dictatorship of Adolf Hitler, who embarked on a gradual conquest of Europe, beginning with the Rhinelands, then Austria, Czechoslovakia, Poland and beyond.

The war and its aftermath again reshaped the geopolitics of Europe, particularly Germany. The country lost land to France and Poland, and its territory was also divided between the winning allies – Britain, France, the USA and the Soviet Union. The German capital, Berlin, was in the Soviet sector, but the city itself was also divided between the four powers.

This division of Germany had important results, and in 1949 the country became two separate states – the German Democratic Republic (East Germany), and the Federal Republic of Germany (West Germany). The former was communist-run and dominated by the Soviet Union, whereas the latter was capitalist and protected by the West. The two Germanies, which remained separate until 1990, were divided by the 'Iron Curtain', one of the strongest political boundaries Europe, and the world, has ever known. It was the product of the so-called Cold War, the name given to the post-war political and economic conflict and rivalry between the USSR and the USA. The main arena for this was Europe, and it led to the east-west division of Europe into ideological, military and economic power blocs.

The Cold War

The damage the Second World War inflicted on Europe's economy, was incalculable. Vast sums of money,

After the shortages of the war and the Russian blockade of goods into Berlin (prompting the Allied airlift), Berliners could buy fruit such as oranges for the first time since 1939.

Czechoslovakia

Whereas Poland's fate was to be caught between Germans and Russians, one of the problems of Czechoslovakia has been its location between Germans and more Germans. Its origin was in Ceské, the area around Prague, which became a state in AD 900. But it was wedged between the two lobes of German lands, which were to become Prussia and Austria. Ceské was annexed by Austria in 1526, but reappeared in 1918 with the carve-up of the Austro-Hungarian Empire. Post-First World War agreements linked the Czechs of Ceské and Moravia with the quite different Slovaks, the Slavic people of Slovakia, leading to internal problems of unity. Occupied by Germany in the Second World War Czechoslovakia, like most East European countries, then came under the domination of the Soviet Union. An attempt to gain a greater measure of independence and freedom was crushed by the Russian invasion of 1968. In 1968 it was a front-line state between NATO forces and those of the Warsaw Pact. Nevertheless, the state established itself as one of the most successful economies in the former Soviet bloc.

The map of Europe before the collapse of the USSR and the Soviet military and economic bloc.

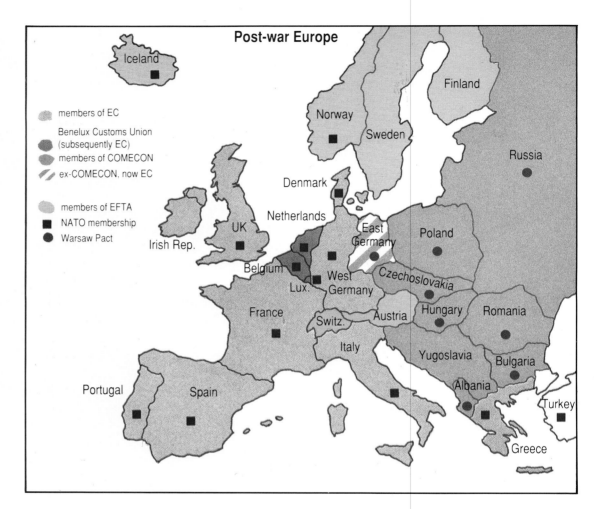

Post-war Europe

members of EC

Benelux Customs Union (subsequently EC)

members of COMECON

ex-COMECON, now EC

members of EFTA

■ NATO membership

● Warsaw Pact

Iceland · Norway · Sweden · Finland · Russia · Denmark · Netherlands · Irish Rep. · UK · Belgium · Lux. · West Germany · East Germany · Poland · Czechoslovakia · Hungary · Romania · France · Switz. · Austria · Yugoslavia · Bulgaria · Italy · Albania · Turkey · Portugal · Spain · Greece

as well as co-operation between nations, were needed to rebuild Europe. The US Secretary of State, George Marshall, devised a European Recovery Programme, known as the Marshall Plan.

The USA was interested in Europe for both political and military reasons. It was fearful of the growing power of the Soviet Union and its control over the states of Eastern Europe. For this reason Marshall Aid was available to non-communist countries only. It was not available to the Soviet Union and its communist allies, which meant that economic recovery in Eastern Europe was much slower.

Founded in 1949, the Council for Mutual Economic Assistance (COMECON) was the East's answer to economic co-operation, but its efficient working was hindered by socialist politics and dictator governments in many East

European countries. As a result, a great economic gulf developed between the capitalist West and the communist East. Many Eastern Europeans moved westwards, as they had frequently done throughout history, and this loss of workforce further undermined the East's recovery programme. The military boundary of the Iron Curtain prevented further migration and it also extended through Berlin as the infamous Berlin Wall which, until 1989, divided the Western from the Soviet Sectors.

Economic associations

Since the end of the Second World War, much of the progress towards European unity has been made through economic-trading associations. This process began with the formation of the 'Benelux' customs union in 1948. In 1951 the European Coal and Steel Community was created, followed (1957) by the European Economic Community (EEC). This founded the European Atomic Energy Community (EURATOM) for the peaceful use of nuclear power. In 1967 these three Communities merged to become the European Community (EC). The EC's major objectives were the removal of all trade barriers between countries and the establishment of complete freedom of movement across borders by workers in search of employment. After 1967 the membership of the EC was considerably enlarged (*page* 45). More countries are seeking membership, and many Eastern European states are interested in joining the free market of the West.

Political unity?

The upheavals and changes in Eastern Europe and the USSR have made European co-operation much more feasible. Communism has now ceased to be a ruling power, even in the old USSR. The three Baltic countries (Soviet until 1991) of Estonia, Latvia and Lithuania have become independent sovereign states. The twelve other former USSR republics are also independent but have grouped themselves under the title of the Commonwealth of Independent States (CIS). The

The chart lists the Commonwealth of Independent States (CIS), which have emerged from the former USSR.

The CIS (former USSR)			
Country	Area (km²)	Population	Capital
Russia	17,075,400	147,386,000	Moscow
Kazakhstan	2,717,300	16,538,000	Alma-Ata
Ukraine	603,700	51,704,000	Kiev
Uzbekistan	494,600	19,906,000	Tashkent
Turkmenia	488,100	3,534,000	Ashkhabad
Byelorussia	207,600	10,200,000	Minsk
Kirghizia	198,500	4,291,000	Fruuze
Tadzhikistan	143,100	5,112,000	Dushanbe
Azerbaijan	86,600	7,029,000	Baku
Georgia	69,700	5,449,000	Tbilisi
Moldavia	33,700	4,341,000	Kishinev
Armenia	29,000	3,283,000	Yerevan

Above **The European Parliament building, Strasbourg. Both the European Court and the Council of Europe, which works for economic and social progress and the preservation of the common European heritage, are based here.**

move in the East is towards a 'market-economy', but this is a difficult task after decades of economic inefficiency. The East is now dependent on the experience and investment of the West and much help is being given, especially in Germany which has acquired the territory and problems of what was the GDR. Another big problem is the ethnic tensions found in many Eastern countries, and the break-up of states. Yugoslavia provides a dramatic example of this 'Balkanization', with its once-federal republics gaining independence by civil war.

In Western Europe, the main move towards unity was the establishment in 1992 of a single European Market. As a result, the barriers to free trading have been removed, as well as the obstacles to the movement of peoples, goods and money. Many Europeans see this as the first step to the growing political unification of Europe. This, they argue, can only be brought about through a Federal Europe. Others are strongly opposed to this development. They see federalism as giving some European countries greater advantages than others.

National identity remains strong throughout Europe, and many argue that it is too complicated an area to produce any lasting form of unity. Nevertheless, much co-operation and change has recently affected Europe and its political map. These events have overcome many divisions and mistrusts inherited from the wars of this century, as well as many of the conflicts which stem from earlier times.

Right **The formation of the EC.**

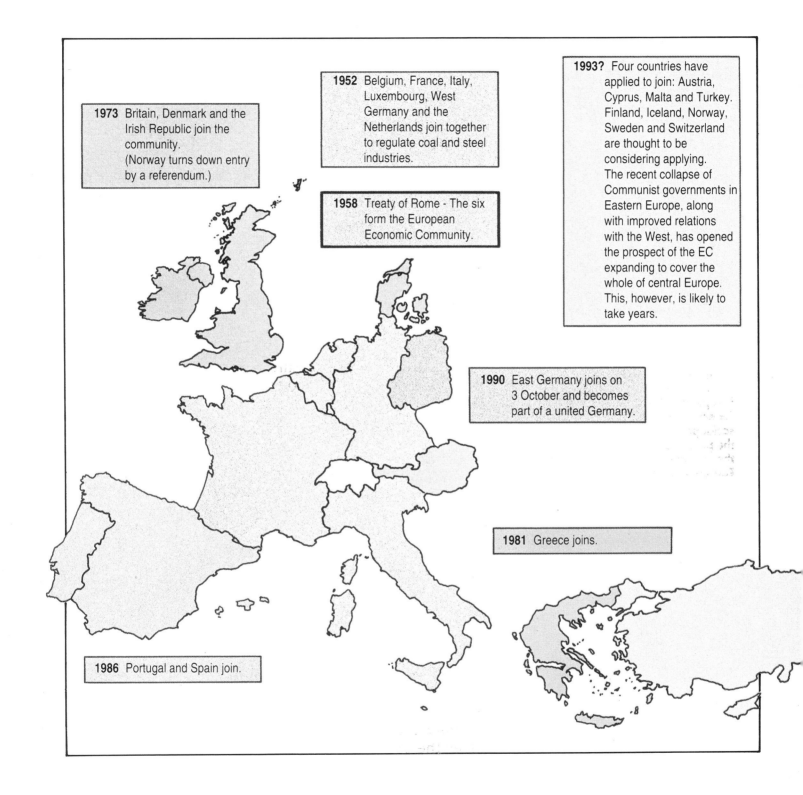

1973 Britain, Denmark and the Irish Republic join the community. (Norway turns down entry by a referendum.)

1952 Belgium, France, Italy, Luxembourg, West Germany and the Netherlands join together to regulate coal and steel industries.

1958 Treaty of Rome - The six form the European Economic Community.

1993? Four countries have applied to join: Austria, Cyprus, Malta and Turkey. Finland, Iceland, Norway, Sweden and Switzerland are thought to be considering applying. The recent collapse of Communist governments in Eastern Europe, along with improved relations with the West, has opened the prospect of the EC expanding to cover the whole of central Europe. This, however, is likely to take years.

1990 East Germany joins on 3 October and becomes part of a united Germany.

1981 Greece joins.

1986 Portugal and Spain join.

Glossary

AUTONOMY The right and freedom of a state, nation or community to self-government.

BALKANIZATION To divide a territory into small warring states, as in the Balkan Peninsula.

BUFFER ZONE OR STATE An area of state, usually neutral, between two rival political powers.

CAPITALISM An economic system based on the private ownership of the methods of production, distribution and exchange.

COMMONWEALTH A group of people, nations or states united by some common interest.

COMMUNISM Belief in a classless society where private ownership has been abolished and the means of production belong to the community.

CONSTITUTION The important and fundamental political principles on which a state is governed.

DEMOCRACY A form of government by the people or their elected representatives.

FEDERALISM The government of a state which is divided between one central and several other regional governments.

GEOPOLITICS The study of the way geographical factors influence politics, especially international politics.

IRREDENTISM The political, often military, fight by people to re-gain lost territory.

MARKET ECONOMY An economy based on the principles of capitalism.

NATION A group of people who are conscious of their individuality or differences from other people.

NATO The North Atlantic Treaty Organization, founded in 1949 by fifteen nations, for purposes of collective security. Original members included the USA, Canada, Iceland and the UK.

OLIGARCHY A form of government where a small group of individuals rule the state.

REPUBLIC A form of government in which the people or their elected representatives hold supreme power.

UNITED NATIONS A powerful association of world countries dedicated to peace-keeping and other forms of global co-operation.

WARSAW PACT A military treaty and economic association of Eastern European countries formed in 1955, now defunct.

Books to read

Britain, Europe and Beyond, 1700-1900, Martin Dickinson (Macmillan Educational, 1982)

British and European History, Ed Rayner (Longman, 1989)

Eighteenth-century Europe, Leonard W. Cowie (HarperCollins, 1970)

Europe in Rivalry and Accord: The Great Powers, 1870-1914, (Hodder Educational, 1990)

European History 1455-1990, Rachel Maund (Routledge, 1992)

European History 1848-1945, T. A. Morris (Collins Educational, 1987)

The European World, 1870-1975, Thomas Kingston Derry (HarperCollins, 1878)

A Family in World War I, Stewart Ross (Wayland, 1987)

The Origins of the Second World War, R. Henig (Routledge, 1985)

The Rise of Fascism, Peter Chrisp (Wayland, 1991)

Spotlight on Medieval Europe, Stewart Ross (Wayland, 1986)

Spotlight on Post-war Europe, Michael Gibson (Wayland, 1986)

Spotlight on Renaissance Europe, Nathaniel Harris (Wayland, 1987)

Success in European History 1815-1941, Jack B. Watson (John Murray, 1981)

Towards European Unity, Stewart Ross (Wayland, 1989)

Unity in Europe, David Hall (Collins Educational, 1987)

Europe's Sovereign States

Country	Area (km²)	Population	Capital	Form of Government
Albania	28,748	3,200,000	Tirana	Republic
Andorra	453	50,000	Andorra La Vella	Principality
Austria	83,853	7,635,600	Vienna	Federal Republic
Belgium	30,519	9,920,000	Brussels	Constitutional Monarchy
Bulgaria	110,912	9,020,000	Sofia	Republic
Cyprus	9,251	696,000	Nicosia	Republic
Czechoslovakia	127,869	15,700,000	Prague	Federal Republic
Denmark	43,075	5,129,000	Copenhagen	Constitutional Monarchy
Estonia	45,100	1,560,000	Tallinn	Republic
Finland	338,107	4,990,000	Helsinki	Republic
France	551,500	56,000,000	Paris	Republic
Germany	387,048	78,850,000	Berlin	Federal Republic
Gibraltar	6.5	31,000	Gibraltar	British Crown Colony
Greece	131,944	10,010,000	Athens	Republic
Hungary	93,032	10,600,000	Budapest	Republic
Iceland	102,829	251,000	Reykjavik	Republic
Irish Republic	70,283	3,700,000	Dublin	Republic
Italy	301,252	57,500,000	Rome	Republic
Latvia	63,700	2,710,000	Riga	Republic
Liechtenstein	160	30,000	Vaduz	Constitutional Monarchy
Lithuania	65,200	3,670,000	Vilnius	Republic
Luxembourg	2,586	375,000	Luxembourg	Constitutional Monarchy
Malta	316	346,000	Valetta	Republic
Monaco	1.95	29,000	Monaco-ville	Constitutional Monarchy
Netherlands	41,548	14,715,000	Amsterdam	Constitutional Monarchy
Norway	323,895	4,240,000	Oslo	Constitutional Monarchy
Poland	312,683	38,390,000	Warsaw	Republic
Portugal	92,082	10,410,000	Lisbon	Republic
Romania	237,500	23,200,000	Bucharest	Republic
San Marino	61	23,000	San Marino	Republic
Spain	504,782	39,800,000	Madrid	Constitutional Monarchy
Sweden	449,964	8,459,000	Stockholm	Constitutional Monarchy
Switzerland	41,293	6,673,200	Berne	Federal Republic
Turkey	779,452	56,800,000	Ankara	Republic
United Kingdom	244,046	57,080,000	London	Constitutional Monarchy
Vatican City	44 Hectares	1,000	Vatican City	Holy See
Yugoslavia	255,804	23,800,000	Belgrade	Federal Republic

INDEX